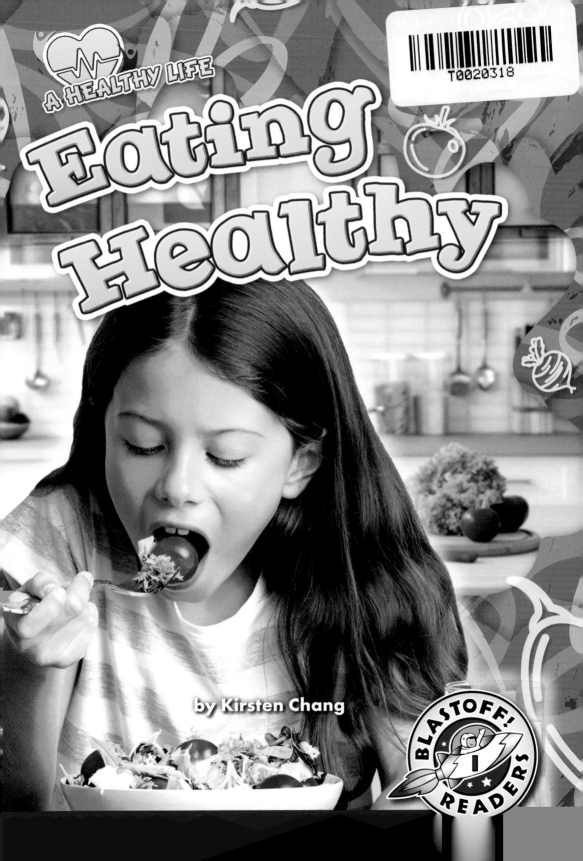

A HEALTHY LIFE

Eating Healthy

by Kirsten Chang

BLASTOFF! READERS

Blastoff! Readers are carefully developed by literacy experts to build reading stamina and move students toward fluency by combining standards-based content with developmentally appropriate text.

 Level 1 provides the most support through repetition of high-frequency words, light text, predictable sentence patterns, and strong visual support.

 Level 2 offers early readers a bit more challenge through varied sentences, increased text load, and text-supportive special features.

 Level 3 advances early-fluent readers toward fluency through increased text load, less reliance on photos, advancing concepts, longer sentences, and more complex special features.

★ **Blastoff! Universe**

Reading Level

Grade **K**

Grades **1–3**

Grade **4**

This edition first published in 2022 by Bellwether Media, Inc.

No part of this publication may be reproduced in whole or in part without written permission of the publisher. For information regarding permission, write to Bellwether Media, Inc., Attention: Permissions Department, 6012 Blue Circle Drive, Minnetonka, MN 55343.

Library of Congress Cataloging-in-Publication Data

Names: Chang, Kirsten, 1991- author.
Title: Eating healthy / Kirsten Chang.
Description: Minneapolis : Bellwether Media, 2022. | Series: A healthy life | Includes bibliographical references and index. | Audience: Ages 5-8 | Audience: Grades K-1 | Summary: "Developed by literacy experts for students in kindergarten through grade three, this book introduces the benefits of eating healthy to young readers through leveled text and related photos"–Provided by publisher.
Identifiers: LCCN 2021041258 (print) | LCCN 2021041259 (ebook) | ISBN 9781644875780 (library binding) | ISBN 9781648346637 (paperback) | ISBN 9781648345890 (ebook)
Subjects: LCSH: Nutrition–Juvenile literature. | Health–Juvenile literature.
Classification: LCC RA784 .C442 2022 (print) | LCC RA784 (ebook) | DDC 613.2–dc23
LC record available at https://lccn.loc.gov/2021041258
LC ebook record available at https://lccn.loc.gov/2021041259

Editor: Rebecca Sabelko   Designer: Andrea Schneider

Printed in the United States of America, North Mankato, MN.

Table of Contents

Lunch Time!

It is lunch time.
Ava takes a bite.
Mmm! Her meal is
full of healthy foods.

Why Is Eating Healthy Important?

Eating **balanced** meals and snacks is important for good health.

Our bodies need **nutrients** to grow and be strong. Healthy foods have more nutrients.

Eating healthy
helps us learn
new things.

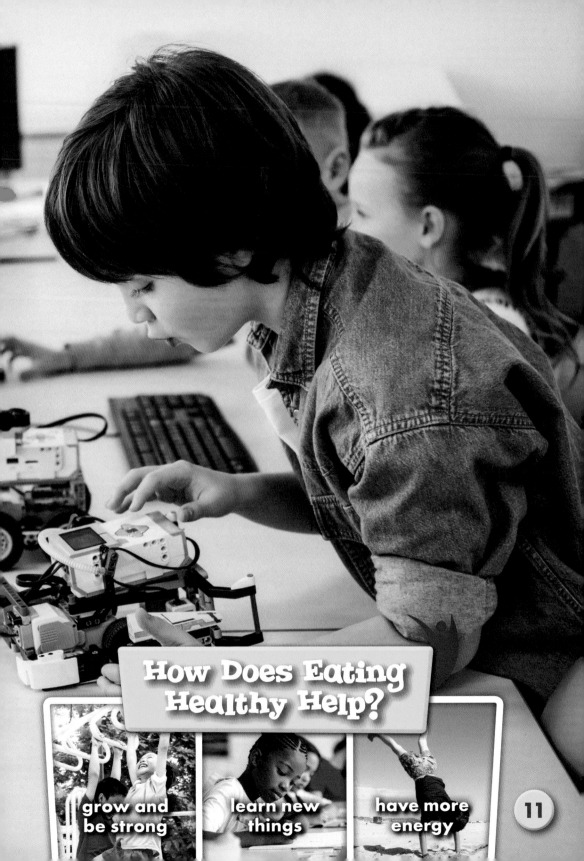

How Does Eating Healthy Help?

grow and be strong

learn new things

have more energy

We feel better when we eat healthy foods. We have more **energy** to play!

Eating unhealthy foods all the time is bad for us.
It can make us sick.

How Do We Eat Healthy?

Emma's lunch has fruits, vegetables, and **whole grains**. It also has **dairy** and **protein**.

Ron eats healthy.
He drinks a lot of water.
But sometimes he has
an unhealthy snack, too.

Tools for Eating Healthy

balanced meals

healthy snacks

water

Eating healthy foods
is good for our bodies!

What healthy foods do you enjoy eating?

Glossary

balanced

has the right amounts of different things

nutrients

things needed for plants or animals to live and grow

dairy

foods that are made from milk

protein

a natural substance in foods such as meat, eggs, and beans

energy

the power to be able to do things

whole grains

foods made from wheat or similar grains that have not been cut up

To Learn More

AT THE LIBRARY

Clark, Rosalyn. *Why We Eat Healthy Foods*.
Minneapolis, Minn.: Lerner Publications, 2018.

MacReady, R. J. *Eating Healthy Foods*.
New York, N.Y.: Cavendish Square Publishing,
2022.

Reinke, Beth Bence. *Healthy Eating Habits*.
Minneapolis, Minn.: Lerner Publications, 2019.

ON THE WEB

FACTSURFER

Factsurfer.com gives you
a safe, fun way to find
more information.

1. Go to www.factsurfer.com.

2. Enter "eating healthy" into
   the search box and click 🔍.

3. Select your book cover to see
   a list of related content.

Index